MW01626069

1000 WORDS

Author and Artist
Wenqing Yan
Yuumei.deviantart.com
Yuumei.Yan@gmail.com

Editor and Publisher
Eric San Gregorio

Layout
Heather Moore

4th Dimension Entertainment®
Website: www.4de.com
Email: info@4de.com

ISBN: 978-0-9819599-9-3
First Printing: February 2012
10 9 8 7 6 5 4 3 2 1
Printed in China

100 WORDS

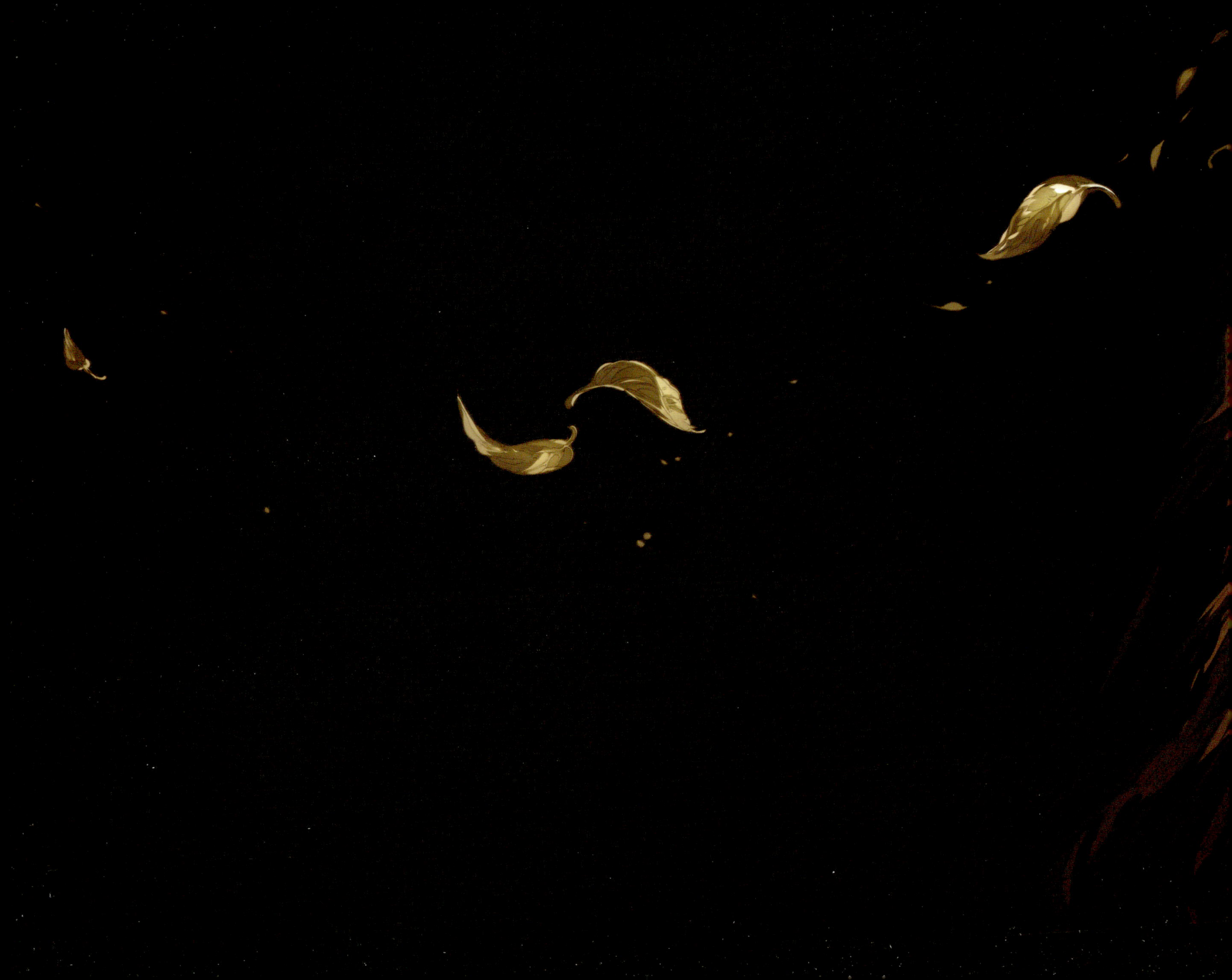

What is it,
little girl?
Mister,
can you teach me
how to draw?

You're really good...

Please teach me.
I want to
draw something...
special...

But the best

I can draw

is this...

That's already very good.
But I want to
be better
like you...
Just practice everyday,
and you will be great
in a few years.

A few years!
It'll be too late by then...

What do you mean by too late,
what will happen?

This...

Mommy and Daddy
have been hurting each other...

After they separate,
I won't be able to draw my family
no matter how good I am.

That's why...

please teach me.

I can't.

It will take years to teach you.

And I'm a traveler. I'll be gone by tomorrow.

would it not be better to have

your family

instead of just a drawing?

I don't want to feel so helpless.

Don't despair.

Someone once told me
art is about content,
not skills.

And a picture is worth
a thousand words.

I have an idea.

Why don't we make
an art trade?

Your drawing *for one thousand words.*

But it's ripped...

And what can I do...

with
one thousand words?

Maybe,
just maybe,
one thousand words will be enough
to convince your parents...

Meet me here tomorrow.
You'll see.

Mister,
You're here!

Of course!

As promised,
one thousand words.

But don't open it.
Give it to...

your parents.

No matter what

the sun will always shine.

Just look for a brighter tomorrow

and you will find...

Mister!

You've grown.

I want to thank you

for helping me!

So your family
is still together.
I'm glad.

They divorced soon after.

I'm sorry...

I failed to make a difference.

That's not true!
You've made a difference
in me.

I've decided to become an artist
like you.
I will make a difference,
and change the world for the better.
One thousand words at a time.

Here,
one thousand words
of my gratitude.

One thousand words

indeed.

Thank you! Thank you! Thank you! Thank you! Thank you!
Thank you! Thank you! Thank you! Thank you! Thank you!
Thank you! Thank you! Thank you! Thank you! Thank you!
Thank you! Thank you! Thank you! Thank you! Thank you!
Thank you! Thank you! Thank you! Thank you! Thank you!
Thank you! Thank you! Thank you! Thank you! Thank you!
Thank you! Thank you! Thank you! Thank you! Thank you!
Thank you! Thank you! Thank you! Thank you! Thank you!
Thank you! Thank you! Thank you! Thank you! Thank you!
Thank you! Thank you! Thank you! Thank you! Thank you!
Thank you! Thank you! Thank you! Thank you! Thank you!
Thank you! Thank you! Thank you! Thank you! Thank you!
Thank you! Thank you! Thank you! Thank you! Thank you!
Thank you! Thank you! Thank you! Thank you! Thank you!
Thank you! Thank you! Thank you! Thank you! Thank you!
Thank you! Thank you! Thank you! Thank you! Thank you!

Thank you! Thank you! Thank you! Thank you! Thank you!
Thank you! Thank you! Thank you! Thank you! Thank you!
Thank you! Thank you! Thank you! Thank you! Thank you!
Thank you! Thank you! Thank you! Thank you! Thank you!
Thank you! Thank you! Thank you! Thank you! Thank you!
Thank you! Thank you! Thank you! Thank you! Thank you!
Thank you! Thank you! Thank you! Thank you! Thank you!
Thank you! Thank you! Thank you! Thank you! Thank you!
Thank you! Thank you! Thank you! Thank you! Thank you!
Thank you! Thank you! Thank you! Thank you! Thank you!
Thank you! Thank you! Thank you! Thank you! Thank you!
Thank you! Thank you! Thank you! Thank you! Thank you!
Thank you! Thank you! Thank you! Thank you! Thank you!
Thank you! Thank you! Thank you! Thank you! Thank you!
Thank you! Thank you! Thank you! Thank you! Thank you!
Thank you! Thank you! Thank you! Thank you! Thank you!

THE
N
D

Thank you!